MEN WHO
SHAPED
AMERICA

MEN WHO SHAPED AMERICA

By
Robert Flood

MOODY PRESS
CHICAGO

© 1976 by
THE MOODY BIBLE INSTITUTE
OF CHICAGO

Library of Congress Cataloging in Publication Data

Flood, Robert.
  Men who shaped America.

    CONTENTS: Christopher Columbus.—William Bradford.
            —John Eliot. [etc.]
    1. Christian biography. 2. United States—
Biography. I. Title.
BR1700.2.F52   920.71'0973   75-34339
ISBN 0-8024-5242-6

First Printing, January 1976, 45,000
Second Printing, January 1976, 10,000
Third Printing, February 1976, 30,000

Printed in the United States of America

Contents

CHAPTER   PAGE

INTRODUCTION   7

Christian men of yesteryear set the stage for today's evangelical resurgence.

1. CHRISTOPHER COLUMBUS   11

What caused this famous Portuguese mariner to sail far into the dark unknown?

2. WILLIAM BRADFORD   18

The governor of Plymouth Colony prompted the American system of free enterprise.

3. JOHN ELIOT   25

He loved the Indians and jumped ahead of his time as a superb linguistic missionary.

4. WILLIAM PENN   30

Christian qualities kept this earnest Quaker from squandering a large piece of real estate.

5. SAMUEL ADAMS   34

Was his part in the Boston Tea Party equal to the role of a modern revolutionist?

6. JOHN WITHERSPOON   40

A minister of the Gospel earned the right to sign the Declaration of Independence.

7. JONATHAN EDWARDS   47

    One of early America's most brilliant men triggered a great revival.

8. FRANCIS ASBURY   55

    No frontiersman traveled so many miles through the wilderness as did this incredible circuit rider.

9. NOAH WEBSTER   62

    He systematized knowledge like a human computer and spent thirty-six years on an American dictionary.

10. FRANCIS SCOTT KEY   66

    The man who penned the words to the *Star Spangled Banner* knew what Christian faith really is.

11. ABRAHAM LINCOLN   70

    Time and time again this great President humbly sought out "the almighty Ruler of Nations."

12. DWIGHT L. MOODY   80

    He preached to one hundred million people and founded an institute that preaches to the world.

CONCLUSION   89

    As in yesteryear, dedicated Christians can shape the America of tomorrow.

NOTES   94

INTRODUCTION

LOOK IN ALMOST EVERY DIRECTION TODAY, and you will find an evangelical renaissance in many communities, on the college campus, even in the corridors of the capitol.

Today evangelical churches thrive, while others struggle for survival. The public press, which little more than a decade or two ago might have simply ignored or ridiculed anything that smacked of fundamentalism, lavishly ballyhooed the "Jesus movement"; and now, with only occasional exception, it treats evangelical Christians with fairness and respect.

Evangelical book sales have flourished in the past few years, some books becoming best sellers on the national scene. Supermarkets and big-name chain stores display the evangelical message, and an average of two new Christian bookstores open every day.

U.S. News and World Report, among other observers, cites a "Boom in Protestant Schools," most of them evangelical.

Thousands of neighborhood Bible-study groups have sprung up in cities and towns across the land.

And there are other such phenomena:

A vigorous "Jews for Jesus" movement (some would prefer the term "Hebrew Christian") surfaces as more and more Jewish people tell of discovering Jesus as their Messiah.

Prominent professional athletes by the score become Christians and "pass it on."

Millions of Americans tune simultaneously to an evangelistic crusade on television.

Student Christian movements flourish on the secular university campus, attracting thousands.

A son of the United States President experiences conversion and heads for an evangelical school.

Businessmen and office workers hold lunch-hour Bible breaks.

A vigorous Christian thrust emerges among airline workers—pilots, stewardesses, mechanics.

Several figures in the Watergate scandal find Jesus Christ as Saviour.

Three astronauts return from the moon and go into full-time evangelism.

While once-prominent liberal seminaries close, evangelical seminaries expand.

As the momentum continues, many who stand outside the evangelical stream look on perplexed.

Let us not forget, however, that today's spiritual surge, whatever its extent, has not erupted out of nowhere. Its foundations, of course, go back far beyond the beginnings of our nation to the events of Calvary and all that followed. In the lifetime of our own nation, faithful Christians have established the foundations, however quietly, for the events of this hour. "One generation shall praise thy works to another" (Psalm 145:4), say the Scriptures, and to all faithful predecessors we must give credit. The evangelical threads of American history still hold, because God has seen to it. "Jesus Christ the same yesterday, and today, and forever" (Hebrews 13:8).

The bicentennial era has produced no shortage of books that attempt to analyze the genius of America. But often even the best books on our American heritage treat the spiritual backdrop inadequately. Even many Evangelicals know amazingly little about the men of spiritual conviction who helped make America.

This book highlights just a few of those men.

ONE

CHRISTOPHER COLUMBUS

CHRISTOPHER COLUMBUS, say most of the history books, discovered the New World. Not everyone thinks so. Nordic mariner Leif Ericson, some insist, arrived first. Others cite a nautical chart, lost for five centuries, which gives evidence that Portuguese captains had found the New World by 1424. And there are at least a score of other speculations.

The debate may never be resolved. But one thing is sure: Columbus was one of the great seamen of all time. As a young lad, while employed making charts and sailing up and down the coasts of Europe and Africa under the Portuguese flag, he began to dream of the "impossible trip."[1]

By this time every educated man knew the world was a sphere. And so they also understood that, theoretically, it would be possible to reach the Orient and its rich trade potential by sailing west. But no one had the courage to prove it. To the west lay a dark, turbulent waste, and who knew how far it might stretch? Little did they suspect that still another continent lay between!

It took Columbus years to gain support for his idea of sailing west, and then to raise the finances for the actual voyage. Queen Isabella of Spain, impressed with Columbus as a person and aware of what the expedition's success could mean to Spain, finally granted the funds.

Columbus put together a small fleet of three ships. If one sank, two would still be near for the rescue. He and his crewmen pushed off from Lisbon, choosing first to run south before the prevailing northerlies to the Canary Islands. There the ships stopped for food and repairs, weighed anchor for the last time in the Old World and headed due west into the dark unknown.

On September 6, 1492, they passed the lofty 12,000-foot peak of Tenerife in the Canary Islands, which remained in sight until September 9. But by nightfall that day every trace of land had sunk below the eastern horizon, and the three ships were alone on an unchartered ocean. Columbus described the course: "West: nothing to the north, nothing to the south."

What really motivated this great explorer to sail off into uncharted waters? Historians have often summed up the early migrations to America as ventures for "God, gold and glory." Where, then, did this man's greatest interests lie?

The sovereigns who underwrote the voyage promised Columbus a healthy 10 percent of the expected profits. But this was not an unusual amount at that time, nor did the profit motive seem to preoccupy him. Some of his ships' crew perhaps, but not so Columbus himself.

Then it must have been the adventure and glory that impelled him. Columbus indeed was equal to the adventure of all adventures, and surely he knew the honors that would be his if he returned home in success.

But was this the whole picture?

Even secular historians acknowledge that Columbus was a devout man with a sense of destiny. But for the most part they have missed or underplayed the greatest single driving force behind the voyage of Columbus: the impact of the Bible upon his life.

August J. Kling, who has researched the subject thoroughly, says that "Columbus' use of the Bible is one of the best documented facts of his remarkable career, but it is one of the least known to the general public."[2]

Christopher Columbus, he says, was a careful student of the Scriptures and of great biblical commentators to which he had access. He used Latin fluently and knew enough elementary Greek and Hebrew to study the exegesis of certain biblical words that were of special interest to him.

For his time he was an unusual self-taught Christian layman. All of Columbus' sailing journals and most of his private letters, observes Kling, give evidence of his biblical knowledge and a genuine love for Jesus Christ.

At this point some will object that Columbus lived under the theology of the Roman church and, indeed, was loyal to it.

But remember, this was still a quarter century before the Reformation. It would have been impossible, then, for Columbus to be a Protestant!

But let Columbus tell the story in his own words. They are translated from the fifteenth-century Spanish introduction to the *Book of Prophecies*, the least known of Columbus's endeavors, yet the only book he ever wrote. Here are some excerpts:

"At a very early age I began to sail upon the ocean. For more than forty years, I have sailed everywhere that people go.

"I prayed to the most merciful Lord about my heart's great desire, and He gave me the spirit and the intelligence for the task: seafaring, astronomy, geometry, arithmetic, skill in drafting spherical maps and placing correctly the cities, rivers, mountains and ports. I also studied cosmology, history, chronology and philosophy.

"It was the Lord who put into my mind (I would feel His hand upon me) to sail from here to the Indies.

"I am a most unworthy sinner, but I have cried out to the Lord for grace and mercy, and they have covered me completely. I have found the sweetest consolation since I made it my whole purpose to enjoy His marvelous presence.

"These are great and wonderful things for the earth, and the signs are that the Lord is hastening the end. The fact that the gospel must still be preached to so many lands in such a short time—this is what convinces me."[3]

Columbus saw the success of his voyage as a direct confirmation of God's will for his life. He saw his discovery as opening up new lands and tribes to the Gospel. And he understood something of how the missionary task—the preaching of the Gospel to the ends of the earth—related to prophecy.

One wonders that, when the ocean waters churned at their worst and his crew threatened mutiny, if Columbus would have made it had he not been driven on by his strong sense of divine mission and destiny.

Only three days away from their landing, his men demanded in anger that the ships turn back. They had not seen land for thirty-one days. Enough of this nightmare to nowhere! But Columbus, in determination, urged them on, with the cry of *"Adelante! Adelante!"* ("Onward") since he "had come to go to the Indies, and so had to continue until he found them, with Our Lord's help."

Some years ago this example of a man who wouldn't quit inspired American poet Joaquin Miller to write his now famous account, "Columbus." Day after day they sailed on, with no sign of land:

> They sailed and sailed, as winds might blow,
>   Until at last the blanched mate said:
> "Why, now not even God would know
>   Should I and all my men fall dead.
> These very winds forget their way,
>   For God from these dread seas is gone.
> Now speak, brave Adm'r'l; speak and say"—
>   He said: "Sail on! sail on! and on!"

No, even in their darkest hour, "God from these dread seas" was *not* gone. Like the disciples on the tumultuous sea of Galilee and Paul in the terrifying storm off Malta, Columbus saw that "the LORD on high is mightier than ... the mighty waves of the sea" (Psalm 93:4).

Columbus and his men finally reached another continent and they called this first land-fall "San Salvador" (Holy Saviour). In February, 1502, while preparing for his fourth voyage, the explorer asked for clergymen to assist him "in the name of the Lord Jesus to spread his name and Gospel everywhere." Columbus specified that he wanted to select these evangelists him-self.

In this ultimate mission, however, he was to face disappointment. Writes Kling: "The sol-diers and adventurers who followed him in later voyages to the new world had little interest in missionary work, in Bible studies or in the preaching of the gospel."[4]

In retrospect, it was fortunate that such a spread of the Gospel awaited another century or more until the Reformation had exploded in southern Europe, spread northward to the British Isles, then jumped across the sea to the North American shore. By this time the "Gos-pel" had been purged of the faulty and extrane-ous trappings which had prompted the furious Martin Luther to hammer his Ninety-five Theses to the door at Wittenburg.

TWO

WILLIAM BRADFORD

WHEN THE PILGRIMS landed in 1620 at Plymouth Rock, they escaped from a treacherous ride on the wild seas only to step into another harrowing experience on the wild land. From the over-populous cabin of the *Mayflower*, they promptly wedged themselves into almost equally crowded forest cabins.

It was not the first permanent English settlement in North America. This honor went to Jamestown, which lay several hundred miles down the Atlantic coast. Jamestown had suffered one catastrophe after another, including a bloody massacre by the Indians just two years before the landing at Plymouth. Time and time again, it seemed, the early Virginia settlers contributed heavily toward their own troubles by selfishness, poor judgment, and lack of discipline.

The Plymouth settlers, like those at Jamestown, also faced great hardship—severe winters, disease, hunger. Three months after the landing, half were dead and most of the others sick.

But there was a different spirit among these of the Plymouth Colony. The difference lay in the extent of their spiritual commitment, an unselfish spirit, discipline, and wise leadership.

William Bradford governed the Plymouth Colony for thirty-seven years, from just a few months after the landing until his death. Bradford was a man of magnanimous spirit, resolute but patient, a man of great spiritual depth, yet neither intolerant nor austere. And had his literary gift not prompted him to write his *History of the Plymouth Plantation*, the world today might have only skimpy evidence of what really happened to those pilgrims back long ago.[1]

From him we have the details of how the few healthy survivors of those first few months in America, among them Miles Standish and William Brewster, assisted the weak "without any grudging in ye least." And there was Squanto, who showed the pilgrims how to plant corn.

William Bradford writes of how the pilgrims rested on God's providence time and time again, "at night not many times knowing wher to have a bitt of anything ye next day. An so, as one well observed, had need to pray that God would give them their dayly brade, above all people in ye world. Yet they bore these wants with great pateince & allacritie of spirite, and that for so long a time as for ye most parte of 2. years."

Bradford's account also describes a three-month drought. The corn withered, the ground cracked. The settlers set aside "a solemne day of humiliation, to seek ye Lord by humble & fervente prayer, in this great distrese."

The Lord answered.

"For all ye morning, and greatest part of the day, it was clear weather & very hotte, and not a cloud or any signe of raine to be seen, yet toward evening it begane to overcast, and shortly after to raine, with shuch sweete and gentel showers, as gave them cause of rejoyceing, & blesing God.

"It came, without either wind, or thunder, or any violence, and by degreese in yt abundance, as that ye earth was thorowly wete and soked therwith. Which did so apparently revive & quicken ye decayed corne & other fruits, as was wonderfull to see, and made ye Indeans astonished to behold; and afterwards the Lord sent them shuch seasonable showers, with enterchange of faire warme weather, as, through his blessing, caused a fruitfull & liberall harvest, to their no small comforte and rejoycing.

"For which mercie (in time conveniente) they also sett aparte a day of thanksgiveing. This being overslipt in its place, I thought meet here to inserte ye same."

And at an earlier time when the crop prospects had looked sorely inadequate these pilgrims made a strategic decision which later proved of great wisdom.

By arrangement with individual "investors" back in England who had underwritten the pilgrim enterprise, the settlers at first ran a "collective" farming operation.

But when an expected shipment of supplies from England failed to materialize, the situation deteriorated. It was then that the pilgrims, under Bradford, "begane to thinke how they might raise as much corne as they could, and obtaine a beter crope then they had done, that they might not still thus languish in miserie."

After much debate they decided that each family should farm its own parcel of land, each operator assuming his own risks and his own potential. The decision violated the agreement and wishes of the shareholders back in England, but it proved a master stroke and, in a sense, established the American system of free enterprise.

"This had very good success," records Bradford, "for it made all hands very industrious, so as much more corne was planted then other waise wold have bene by any means ye Govr or any other could use, and saved him a great deall of trouble, and gave farr better contente."

The collective or socialistic approach, observed the pilgrims in retrospect, squelched incentive, bred confusion and discontent, and retarded "much imploymet that would have been to their benefite and comforte. For ye yong-men that were most able and fitte for labour & service did repine that they should spend their time & streingth to worke for other mens wives and children, with out any recompence.

"The experience ... may well evince," wrote Bradford, "the vantie of that conceite of Platos & other ancients, applauded by some of later times;—that ye taking away of propertie, and bringing in comunitie into a comone wealth, would make them happy and florishing; as if they were wiser then God."

Settlers at Jamestown had made the same discovery during a period of peace secured by an alliance with Powhatan. They discarded their own brand of communism for private enterprise. Joint labor, the common storehouse, and equal distribution went out the window. Sir Thomas Dale broke up land into small lots and granted property rights. Production spiraled.

But in their case, success backfired when overzealous planters put most of their land into tobacco, a crop newly introduced with a good market in England, and neglected the staple crops necessary for survival.

Apart from the beginnings of American private enterprise, the pilgrims at Plymouth, through the Mayflower Compact, also laid the foundations of law and order and established the first "Civil Body Politic" in America.

They could not have foreseen, of course, any long-range significance at the time, for it was intended only as a temporary compact to keep law and order among themselves in a wilderness where there was no law.

At the heart of the compact lay an undisputed conviction that God must be at the center of all law and order and that law without a moral base is really no law at all. The compact also rested on a "covenant" agreement, and this was later to help lay the foundations of American democracy. In other words, all laws and obedience to them would rest not upon a monarchy or a dictatorship, but upon "the consent of the governed."

The Mayflower Compact served Plymouth well for more than seventy years until 1691 when the colony united with Massachusetts.

William Bradford's Plymouth account reveals

time and time again that, despite great hardships, the pilgrims also saw great blessings, and they were a thankful people. In the concluding pages of the drama, Bradford makes the point well:

"God, it seems, would have all men to behold and observe such mercies and works of his providence as these are towards his people, that they in like cases might be incouraged to depend upon God in their trials."

THREE

JOHN ELIOT

IN PURITAN NEW ENGLAND the Bible and education went hand in hand, and an unusually high proportion of the early colonists were university graduates. Not long after they began to settle the Massachusetts Bay Colony these energetic Puritans laid the foundations for both lower and higher education in America.

At the core of the elementary program stood the historic *Bay Psalm Book*, assembled by Richard Mather and John Eliot, two of Puritanism's most illustrious figures. Eliot also distinguished himself as pastor of the church in Roxbury for fifty-seven years.

The name of John Eliot, though, went in the history books not so much for his part in the *Bay Psalm Book*, nor for his more than a half century of service in Roxbury. Rather, he became known for his incredible dedication as a missionary to the Indians.

John Eliot indeed took to heart the evangelistic intent behind the Massachusetts Bay charter. He held the Bible as the literal word of God, the ultimate source of all knowledge, and the Indian as a human being who needed to hear its message. As he wrote in later years: "Pity to the poor Indians, and desire to make the name of Christ chief in these dark ends of the earth—and not the rewards of men—were the very first and chief moves, if I know what did first and chiefly move in my heart, when God was pleased to put upon me that work of preaching to them."[1]

The tribes along Massachusetts Bay spoke Algonquian, a Mahican dialect. Eliot began to explore how he might reach them, and before long concluded that he must learn their language.

His key contact proved to be an Indian named Cockenoe, who had been captured in the Pequot War of 1637 and later put to work for a Dorchester planter. Cockenoe could speak and even read English.

With this helper, and later his replacement, Eliot began the tedious task of analyzing this Indian language. The Algonquian had a habit of compressing complex ideas into extended single words.

After two years he had translated the Ten Commandments and the Lord's Prayer and could speak Algonquian with hesitation. Cotton Mather declared to Eliot that surely it would be easier to teach the Indians English and then preach the Gospel, but Eliot insisted that they should hear the Good News in their native tongue. Eliot would surely have earned the esteem of the thousands of Wycliffe translators today who are at work in similar linguistic missions around the world.

That opportunity came on a chilly October day when a peaceful Indian named Waban led Eliot and three companion clergymen into a wigwam along the river a few miles above Cambridge. There at the council fire Eliot preached the first Protestant sermon in the Indian tongue on the North American continent. He took Ezekiel 27:9 as his text. It proved a good choice. The Indians listened intently, some curious, some doubting, a few malicious. Later, around their smoldering fires, they would ask such questions as:

"Why does not God who has full power kill the Devil that makes all men so bad?"

"Was the Devil or man made first?"

"Why do Englishmen kill all snakes?"

But eventually Waban became a staunch convert to Jesus Christ, as did other Indians. Eliot later gave them clothing, blankets, spades, axes, and other tools. He gave the squaws spinning wheels. The Indians laid out streets and fenced and planted their fields. They became known as the "Praying Indians."

But not all the white settlers, on guard as they were, trusted Eliot's "praying Indians," and others wondered if this missionary work was worth the money spent to reach them. As the Indians prospered, Eliot pressed for ten years to translate the entire Bible into Algonquian, sentence by sentence, verse by verse.

"With his other burdens," observes author Francis Russell, "it is a marvel that he found time to carry on his translating. For in all weathers and all seasons he made his visitation in the towns and friendly settlements, sometimes as far as sixty miles afield. An indomitable figure who could bend to a nor'easter and yet not draw back, who did not hesitate in a pinch to adopt Indian dress, who would stop on a rainy night at any wigwam and wring the water from his socks and be off the next morning."[2]

Some of Eliot's Indian converts became teachers and ministers. His work triggered formation of a London corporation called "the Society for Promoting and Propagating the Gospel of Jesus Christ in New England." His "reports from the mission field" eventually became known as the Indian Tracts. Eliot's Algonquian

Bible, the *Up-Biblum*, finally came off the Cambridge Press at Harvard in 1663, and 200 copies bound in stout leather were released for immediate use of the Indians. It was the first Bible printed in America, and the earliest example in history of the translation and printing of the entire Bible as a means of evangelism.

In later years the outbreak of King Philip's War and unfortunate events that followed the conflict destroyed the Indian work, but many remained loyal to the end. They shall be among those of "every tribe, and tongue, and nation" whom we shall see someday. "He that hath the Son hath life" (1 John 5:12). As one writer said of John Eliot himself as he came to the end of a long and dedicated life, "For him the Great Perhaps was a certainty."

FOUR

WILLIAM PENN

THE RELIGIOUS LIBERTY for which early church-state separatists like Roger Williams and others opted became reality as settlers pushed inland. New colonies like Pennsylvania, New Jersy, and Delaware emerged. In this movement, William Penn stands out as a giant for his influence and vision in the arena of religious freedom.

In England in 1670 William Penn had just received a very large inheritance from his father, Admiral William Penn, who, among other things, had discovered the island of Bermuda. In addition, he was due a settlement of a debt of 16,000 pounds due the estate of his father from the crown.

For this settlement Penn conceived the idea of obtaining a grant of land in America. He petitioned the king for a tract of land "lying north of Maryland, on the east bounded with Delaware River, on the West limited as Mary-

land is, and northward to extend as far as plant-
able, which is altogether Indian."

The venture might at first sound like the
spoiled son out to spend his father's wealth on a
wild speculative scheme. But note the young
man's driving motive as he writes to a friend:

"Because I have been somewhat exercised at
times about the nature and end of government
among men, it is reasonable to expect that I
should endeavor to establish a just and righ-
teous one in this province, that others may take
example by it,—truly this my heart desires. For
the nations want a precedent.... I do, therefore,
desire the Lord's wisdom to guide me, and
those that may be concerned with me, that we
do the thing that is truly wise and just."[1]

Penn said, "I do not find a model in the world
that time, place and some singular emergencies
have not necessarily altered, nor is it easy to
frame a civil government that shall serve all
places alike. I know what is said by the several
admirers of monarchy, aristocracy, and democracy, which are the rule of one, a few, and
many, and are the three common ideas of government when men discourse on that subject.
But I choose to solve the controversy with this
small distinction, and it belongs to all three—
any government is free to the people under it
(whatever be the frame) where the laws rule and

the people are a party to those laws; and more than this is tyranny, oligarchy, or confusion."[2]

As Penn set sail on his return to America from England, where he acquired the Pennsylvania charter, he wrote a moving letter to his family, knowing that with a perilous ocean journey ahead he might not see them again. To his children, specifically, he wrote:

"And as for you who are likely to be concerned in the government of Pennsylvania and my parts of East Jersey, especially the first, I do charge you before the Lord God ... that you be lowly, diligent, and tender, fearing God, loving the people, and hating covetousness." He signed the letter, "Yours as God pleaseth, in that which no waters can quench, no time forget, nor distance wear away."[3]

Clearly Penn saw his new land acquisition as a trust from God. "I eyed the Lord in obtaining it," he wrote, "and more was I drawn inward to look to him, and to owe it to his hand and power than to any other way. I have so obtained it, and desire to keep it that I may not be unworthy of his love."[4]

William Penn, who had become a Quaker, deplored bias and had a keen social conscience. The king gave to him what later became one of the largest states in the northeast United States, with the right to govern. A year later the Duke of York gave Penn what is now Delaware.

A lesser man might have squandered this large piece of real estate to the detriment of generations to come, if not the nation itself. But not Penn. He perceived that the God who had "given it me through many difficulties, will, I believe, bless and make it the seed of a nation."

Into this territory of liberty later poured the sons and daughters of many nations—the Dutch, the Swedes, the Welsh, English Quakers, several German groups, and, last of all, the Scotch-Irish.

With Pennsylvania (Penn's woods) as his model, William Penn not only established a land of liberty, but he advertised it far and wide. What began as simply miles of forest stretching from Philadelphia to Pittsburg soon accommodated peoples of all kind—the persecuted from Europe, the smaller Protestant sects, Catholics, Jews.

Not a few of these settlers abused their liberties. At one point Penn observed that "liberty without obedience is confusion, and obedience without liberty is slavery." But Penn's "Holy Experiment," despite some disappointments to him personally, survived to become a major cornerstone in the foundation of America.

FIVE

SAMUEL ADAMS

ON A CRISP NIGHT in December, 1774, three ship-loads of tea from England drifted restlessly at their moorings in Boston Harbor. The colonists liked their tea, but they were not about to let these merchants of the British East-India Company unload their cargo. England had just imposed a three-cents-a-pound duty, and Americans saw this scheme as both a monopoly and "taxation without representation."

But the tension had been building for a long time. It began after the French and Indian War, when England barred her growing colonies from settling lands beyond the Allegheny Mountains. And when Britain levied heavy taxes on her colonies but failed to seat their representatives in Parliament. And when the Americans were forced to "quarter" English troops in their homes, and when men like Franklin, Jefferson, and Adams became convinced that Britain had usurped many of the colonists' rights.

Tea-laden ships from the same English convoy had also put in at the ports of New York, Philadelphia, and Charleston. They too were refused permission to unload.

This determined stance triggered exultation throughout the colonies and united the American patriots behind the cause of liberty as had no event to that hour.

If any one man's influence triggered the Boston Tea Party, it would have to be that of Samuel Adams. History labels him the "Father of the American Revolution." People everywhere also knew him for his integrity. American historian George Bancroft said of him: "The austere purity of his life witnessed the sincerity of his profession. Evening and morning his house was a house of prayer; and no one more revered the Christian sabbath. He was a tender husband, an affectionate parent."[1]

Adams was not simply a rabble-rouser nor an irresponsible revolutionist intent on tearing down the system. Thomas Jefferson once said of him that "his feet were ever in the stirrup, his lance ever in its rest."[2]

But Samuel Adams had been telling his countrymen for years that America had to take her stand against tyranny. He regarded individual freedom as "the law of the Creator" and a Christian right documented in the New Testament.

And he insisted that his fellow colonists should reason out these inherent Christian rights in the free marketplace where people could discuss, dispute, debate. And so over the years prior to the Revolution he took a vigorous role in the Boston Town Meeting, and encouraged his fellowmen to do likewise. He also established "committees of correspondence" to spread by letter the ideas of liberty throughout the colonies. But he stressed "constitutional principles" rather than "issues" so that people might ultimately act through lawful means, not by riot and rebellion.

What then of the Boston Tea Party which Adams and thousands of others applauded? To some today it comes off as an act of violence akin to those perpetrated by modern-day revolutionists, and not a few have exploited this historical event to justify their anarchy.

But the Boston Tea Party was nothing of the kind. No one was injured; no one harmed. The protesters destroyed no property but the tea itself, which the colonists later offered to pay for.

Nor did the crowds watching from shore seize the occasion to vandalize the town. "The whole," Hutchinson wrote, "was done with very little tumult."[3] The town was never more still on a Saturday night than it was at ten o'clock that evening.

But men from Boston carried the news to other villages throughout the colonies: Boston had stood her ground against the growing British threat to liberty.

Among those on guard at the Boston Harbor that eventful night was John Hancock, a close compatriot of Adams. Both men were later to put their signatures on the Declaration of Independence. Hancock stood by with others, watching the tea spill into the waters, and rejoiced!

It was Hancock and Adams whom the British promptly labeled as their two most wanted men. On the night of Paul Revere's famous midnight ride they were sleeping at the home of a Rev. Jonas Clark in Lexington. Revere arrived about midnight, having narrowly escaped British capture earlier in the evening, to find a colonial guard of eight men stationed on the premises for the protection of Hancock and Adams.

He requested admittance but the sergeant in charge replied that the family had retired and had asked that they might not be disturbed by any noise about the house.

"Noise!" replied Revere, "You'll have noise

enough before long. The Regulars are coming out!"

He got in.

At daybreak the guard ushered Adams and Hancock off to a nearby village, their safety regarded as being of utmost importance. As they passed through the fields while the sunlight glistened in the dew of the fresh morning, Adams sensed the dawn of a nation and exclaimed, "O! what, a glorious morning is this!"

Later in Independence Hall, only hours before the signing of the Declaration of Independence, he would remark to Benjamin Rush: "If it were revealed to me that nine hundred Americans out of every thousand will perish in a war for liberty, I would vote for that war rather than see my country enslaved. The survivors of such a war, though few, would propagate a nation of free men."[4]

The same morning that Hancock and Adams made their escape, a militia of minutemen and the British confronted each other on the nearby Lexington village green. The minutemen held their fire. Suddenly the British let go a deadly volley of fire.

It was a "shot heard 'round the world."[5]

The inevitable American Revolution against the hand of tyranny had begun. After the battles of Lexington and Concord, the British retreated to nearby Boston where, at high cost, they dislodged the colonial militia in the Battle of Bunker Hill. Colonial troops also suffered defeat in the Quebec Campaign. But despite these initial blows, the flame of the Revolution could not be snuffed out, and a momentous act of independence lay just around the corner.

SIX

JOHN WITHERSPOON

THE DECLARATION OF INDEPENDENCE went out over such famous names as Franklin, Jefferson, Hancock, and John and Samuel Adams. Among the fifty-odd legislators who gathered to hammer out this great document of freedom was just one clergyman, John Witherspoon.[1]

Only a few short years before, the gifted preacher and educator had been called over from Scotland to head the College of New Jersey (now Princeton). He was a strong family man with a deep prayer life, which included a day set apart with his household the last day of every year for fasting, humiliation, and prayer.

As war shadows thickened in the American colonies, Congress had seen the seriousness of the situation and designated May 17, 1776, as a day of national fasting and prayer. They asked John Witherspoon to deliver the sermon. And so he did, speaking solemnly on "The Dominion of Providence over the Affairs of Men." He based his views squarely on Scripture and spoke of God's eternal purpose as unfolded in the drama of historical development and delineated the issues of liberty as he saw them.

In a short time Witherspoon had gained such respect, both as a college president and keen political observer, that New Jersey elected him delegate to the 1776 Continental Congress.

Witherspoon felt strongly that ministers of the Gospel should not become entangled in civil affairs. "When our blessed Saviour says, 'My kingdom is not of this world,' " he once preached, "he plainly intimates to his disciples that they have no title to intermeddle with state affairs."

But as a Christian citizen, Witherspoon accepted the challenge.

War clouds hung heavily over the colonies on July 1, 1776, and rain clouds dropped a downpour on the Philadelphia meeting site. Promptly at 9 o'clock John Hancock called the congress to order. But Witherspoon—along with the four other New Jersey delegates—did not show.

By afternoon the question of whether or not to declare independence at this hour stood in doubt. Those against it had marshaled their arguments; and, in spite of a prodeclaration speech by John Adams, who was not known for his strong oratory, the outcome was still in doubt.

At that moment the door opened to admit the delegation from New Jersey.

"We are sorry to be late," said Witherspoon. "We have been held up by the storm."

They shed their wet greatcoats and formally enrolled.

"May we ask for a review of the arguments," Witherspoon said.

No answer.

He repeated his request.

"You already know the arguments," John Adams said.

"That is true but we have not heard them *in Congress.*"

Adams began to review the case. As he did so, he sensed the New Jersey delegation's impatience for independence. Their moral support seemed to give Adams new life. He ended in a burst of eloquence.

Witherspoon jumped to his feet and called out, "New Jersey is plump for independence."

"The oratory is fine but the facts show we're not ripe for it," said John Alsop of New York.

Granite-faced John Witherspoon fixed his flashing eyes on Alsop and thundered, "We are more than ripe for it, and some of us are in danger of rotting for want of it!"

"Hear, hear!" roared Samuel Adams.

"Hear, hear!" rang out from all sections of the room.

Someone called for a trial vote.

Nine delegations voted for adoption of the declaration, two against, one undecided, one abstained.

But final action would wait another three days. Meanwhile, the congress feverishly worked over the proposed Articles of Confederation and took time to hear reports from the battlefield.

On July 4 the document was ready for final vote. But a few of the most cautious delegates still wondered, not about independence itself, but about the timing.

John Witherspoon put their fears to rest.

"There is a tide in the affairs of men," he said. "We perceive it now before us. To hesitate is to consent to our own slavery. That noble instrument should be subscribed to this very morning by every pen in this house. Though these gray hairs must soon descend to the sepulchre, I would infinitely rather that they descend thither by the hand of the executioner than desert at this crisis the sacred cause of my country."

No one spoke.

John Hancock ordered a reading of the final draft:

"When, in the course of human events, it becomes necessary for one people to dissolve the political bands which have connected them with another, and to assume, among the powers of the earth, the separate and equal station to which the laws of nature and of nature's God entitle them, a decent respect to the opinions of mankind, requires that they should declare the causes which impel them to the separation.

"We hold these truths to be self-evident: that all men are created equal, that they are endowed by their Creator with certain inalienable rights; that among these are life, liberty, and the pursuit of happiness. That to secure these rights, governments are instituted among men, deriving their just powers from the consent of the governed; that whenever any form of government becomes destructive of these ends, it is the right of the people to alter or abolish it, and to institute a new government, laying its foundation on such principles, and organizing its powers in such form, as to them shall seem most likely to effect their safety and happiness."

Secretary Charles Thomson called for the vote, starting with the New England colonies and moving south. One "aye" followed another. It was unanimous.

A reverent hush fell over the hall. Some looked out the window. Some prayed.

The secretary placed the document on the speaker's table and looked at the president of the congress. He fingered his goose-quill pen. Then with a flourish and bold strokes John Hancock put his signature on one of the greatest papers of all time.

"There," he said with a smile. "His Majesty can now read my name without glasses. And he can also double the price on my head."

The final signed draft was sent to the printer and, contrary to tradition, it was not signed by others until July 8, nor was it announced publicly until then. Among those signers, of course, was John Witherspoon, who by God's providence had found himself in the right place at the right time.

Outside in the streets of Philadelphia, people gathered in clusters, anxious to learn the decision.

In the steeple of the old State House was a bell on which, by a happy coincidence, was inscribed, "Proclaim liberty throughout all the land unto all the inhabitants thereof."

In the morning the bell ringer went to his post, having placed his boy below to await the announcement, that his bell might be the first to peal forth the glad tidings.

He waited long as the deliberations continued. Impatiently the old man shook his head and repeated, "They will never do it! They will never do it!"

Suddenly he heard his boy clapping his hands and shouting, "Ring! Ring!"

Grasping the iron tongue, he swung it to and fro, proclaiming the glad news of liberty to all the land.

The crowded streets caught up the sound. Every steeple reechoed it.

All that night, by shouts and illuminations and booming of cannon, the people declared their joy.

SEVEN

JONATHAN EDWARDS

MOST HISTORIANS AGREE that Jonathan Edwards stands with Benjamin Franklin as "one of the two outstanding minds in the America of the eighteenth century." Writes biographer Courtney Anderson, "Many believe that in another environment he could have become a scientist greater than Franklin. Certainly as a philosopher and theologian he had no peer in his own time."[1]

Edwards entered Yale at thirteen and graduated valedictorian at seventeen. As he grew in his Christian faith at Yale he became somewhat of a "mystic," in the better sense, in his quest to know more of God. For example, he cites how, on one occasion, he was overwhelmed by reading the words of 1 Timothy 1:17: "Now unto the King eternal, immortal, invisible, the only wise God, be honour and glory for ever and ever. Amen."

"As I read the words, there came into my soul, and was as it were diffused through it, a sense of the glory of the Divine Being; a new sense, quite different from any thing I ever experienced before.... I thought with myself, how excellent a Being that was, and how happy I should be, if I might enjoy that God ... and be as it were swallowed up in him for ever!

"From about that time, I began to have a new kind of apprehensions and ideas of Christ, and the work of redemption, and the glorious way of salvation by him.

"God's excellency, his wisdom, his purity and love, seemed to appear in every thing; in the sun, moon, and stars; in the clouds, and blue sky; in the grass, flowers, trees; in the water, and all nature; which used greatly to fix my mind."[2]

Edwards fell in love with a prominent young Christian lady, Sarah Pierrepont, who was noted for her charm, her flashing wit, and a joyous repartee. She proved the ideal pastor's wife for Edwards, who took over his father-in-law's prestigious pulpit in Northhampton, Massachusetts, two years after their marriage.

The Edwardses eventually raised a remarkably fine family of eleven children. One writer describes the hospitality of the Edwardses as "amazing to us with our more isolated family life. There might be a dozen to eighteen at dinner after a meeting. Guests sometimes stayed for weeks. If they fell ill, they had to be cared for until they were well. They came on horseback, and the horses had to be stabled and cered for. When a guest left, Jonathan usually rode a few miles with him to see him well on his way."[3]

Edwards came to Northhampton at a time when spirituality was at a low ebb. The conditions he describes among the young people might sound much like conditions of today:

"Licentiousness for some years greatly prevailed among the youth of the town; there were many of them very much addicted to night walking and frequenting the tavern, and lewd practices wherein some by their example exceedingly corrupted others. It was their manner to get together in assemblies of both sexes, for mirth and jollity, which they called frolics; and they would often spend the greater part of the night in them, without regard to order in the families they belong to; indeed family government did too much fail in the town."[4]

Then revival began in 1734 while Jonathan Edwards was preaching a series of sermons on justification by faith alone. Conversions began, first the young, then their elders. A notorious young woman was saved. It was like a "flash of lightning" to the young people.

There were those who agonized, and those who rejoiced. Wrote Edwards: "In the spring and summer following, anno 1735, the town seemed to be full of the presence of God; it never was so full of love, nor of joy, and yet so full of distress, as it was then."[5]

By 1736 Edwards' church had 300 new converts, and news of the revival had spread throughout New England.

It took a new surge when George Whitefield arrived from England in 1740 for two years of evangelism in America. Whitefield had already risen to prominence as a key figure in the Wesleyan revivals which were under way in England, a great movement of God triggered there by a group of Christian students at Oxford University.

In those days evangelists did not enjoy the advantage of microphones, but Whitefield didn't need one. At Bristol, England, he had preached to 20,000 at one gathering and all could hear. In America he preached to 5,000 on Boston Common and to 8,000 at one time in the fields. And even at Harvard they received him well, though some held doubts.

In New England the revival reached its peak in 1741, and it was in July at Enfield, Massachusetts, that Edwards preached his most famous sermon, "Sinners in the Hands of an

Angry God." Literally millions first read this classic in a high school or college literature text. It might come as a surprise to many that he did not deliver this sermon in what some would describe as a loud "hellfire and damnation" style. Edwards did not raise his voice nor even move his arms, though his typically good diction and enunciation made every word ring clear. As he hammered home the judgment of God, point upon point, each listener felt the impact of his own guilt.

Was this really the same Jonathan Edwards who spoke so frequently on the love and grace and beauty and majesty of God?

Yes, because Edwards became convinced that one could not really understand the great love of God until he also understood the awfulness of sin. There was such conviction of sin that Edwards had to wait some time until the congregation quieted down. He finally prayed, descended from the pulpit, and talked with the people. They closed with a hymn and then were dismissed.

During little more than two years, from 1740 to 1742, some 25,000 to 50,000 people were added to the New England churches, out of a total population of only 300,000! The movement changed the entire moral tone of New England for the better and justly earned the name of a "Great Awakening."

In time Edwards's soul-searching sermons cut too deeply even for many members of his own congregation at Northhampton, and in 1750 his church, engulfed in controversy by troublemakers, dismissed him from the pulpit. Edwards preached his last sermon there without spirit of revenge, then he launched into a missionary work among the Indians in Stockbridge, a lazy little village in a remote section of Massachusetts. Academic colleagues accused him of wasting his great intellectual abilities in the wilderness, where he would find only savages and the poorly educated. But in this quiet setting Edwards, over a period of seven years, wrote several books in the field of theology that were to influence generations to come. Meanwhile, he won the confidence of the Indians and made a great impact on them. Despite his high intellect, he knew how to preach the simple Gospel.

No doubt his interest in the Indians had been stimulated by the unusual young man who had almost become his son-in-law, David Brainerd.

A student at Yale when the "First Great Awakening" was sweeping New England, David Brainerd at first proved a rebel toward religion. But he did an abrupt about-face after a spiritual experience during "a walk in the woods." Brainerd soon dedicated himself to an unbelievably strenuous work among New England Indian tribes, despite severe tuberculosis. He saw many Indians converted. But five years after his Yale turnabout, the young evangelist died at the home of Jonathan Edwards, to whose lovely daughter Jerusha he was engaged to be married.

Soon after the death Jonathan Edwards published an account of young Brainerd, together with his diary. The book so revealed Brainerd's character and dedication that it became a powerful influence on many lives on behalf of the missions cause, even to this day. As one historian put it, "David Brainerd dead was a more potent influence for the missionary cause in general than was David Brainerd alive."

Incidentally, another of Jonathan Edwards's daughters married the first president of Princeton, and a third married Timothy Dwight, who was to exercise a profound Christian influence as president of Yale. One-third of the Yale student body professed conversion after one of Dwight's chapel messages which brilliantly defended the Christian faith.

And what became of Jonathan Edwards himself? One of his chief critics who had given him such grief at Northhampton finally apologized. The board of Princeton called Edwards out of the wilderness to become president of the college. Only a few months after he assumed office, smallpox took his life during an epidemic. But Jonathan Edwards had already stirred early America to its very foundations through the power of God.

EIGHT

FRANCIS ASBURY

NO PIONEER PREACHER, if indeed any American frontiersman, traveled so many miles through the wilderness in one lifetime, nor endured such hardships, as did the incredible Methodist circuit rider, Francis Asbury.[1] An Englishman by birth, Asbury worked as a blacksmith. He became a Christian at the age of sixteen. When John Wesley called for volunteer evangelists, Asbury set sail for the American colonies in 1771, just five years before the birth of the American nation.

When the American Revolution broke out, Wesley and his missionaries promptly retreated to their native England. All, that is, except Francis Asbury. He saw a job to do, and at heart he was already too much a part of the American scene to abandon its land and its people. He developed a strong love and patriotism for the new nation. His high regard for George

Washington, whom he knew personally, was exceeded perhaps only by his admiration of John Wesley. When the war ceased, he intensified his consuming passion to evangelize the American wilderness, a task that would stretch over forty-four years and an astounding number of miles.

Though a robust man in general, Asbury suffered from one chronic ailment after another, so much so that one biographer calls him a "Job of old on horseback." Migraine headaches plagued him throughout his life, and chronic throat infections would become so severe that doctors feared he would strangle. He wrestled with malaria, asthma, pneumonia, rheumatism, high fevers, and other diseases, and in his mid-forties he plunged onward, convinced he could not live another year. But he lived to the age of seventy-one.

The Journal and Letters of Francis Asbury, a terse daily diary which Asbury kept as he traveled his circuit of some nineteen states, gives some feel of his life that became almost routine. On his long circuit out of West Virginia into Maryland and Pennsylvania in June, 1784, Asbury wrote:

"Although my body is weak, my soul is filled with love to God.... We began to ascend the Alleghany ... keeping the route of Braddock's road for about twenty-two miles, along a rough pathway: arriving at a small house and halting for the night, we had, literally to lie as thick as three in a bed."

And in April of 1790, from Kentucky, where he saw the graves of twenty-four men and women who had been slain by Indians:

"We are now in a house in which a man was killed by savages;... I consider myself in danger; but my God will keep me whilst thousands pray for me." Often he found himself "strangely outdone for want of sleep, having been greatly deprived of it in my journey through the wilderness; which is like being at sea, in some respects, and in others worse. Our way is over mountains, steep hills, deep rivers, and muddy creeks; a thick growth of reeds for miles together; and no inhabitants but wild beasts and savage men ... we ate no regular meal; our bread grew short, and I was much spent."[2]

With his incredible travels which spanned more than four decades, Asbury, perhaps more than any other man, saw firsthand the early nation unfold. He saw the untouched regions beyond the Appalachians (which he called "the American Alps") as lands of future progress and exclaimed in 1803 as he looked over Ohio, "What will not a little enterprise do for a man in this highly favored country!" The next year in

Tennessee he saw the crowds of people moving toward the fertile West and predicted that despite sufferings and hardship, "In ten years, I think, the new State will be one of the most flourishing in the Union."

His journal records the natural wonders of the new nation. In West Virginia, Asbury visited a cave where he saw "some of the greatest natural curiosities my eyes ever beheld," and in one lofty underground chamber he sang "Still out of the Deepest Abyss" and described the sound as "wonderful."

He prayed and sang in the caves, in the valleys, and on the mountaintops. He preached, prayed, and sang in homes, courthouses, barns, and churches. He was a Johnny Appleseed of the Gospel, planting here and there, returning year after year to an abundant harvest. He probably traveled more than one quarter million miles, preached some 25,000 sermons, and may have written around 50,000 letters!

Perhaps because so many knew him and were praying for him, Asbury always seemed to remain unscathed. At the outset of his career he survived a violent sickness on the seas enroute from England. During the American Revolution he remained free from arrest, seemingly an Englishman accepted by the "enemy," and, in the words of one observer, "a lone rider molested on a thousand wilderness trails by neither Indians or bandits."

Asbury set an unbelievable pace for himself, and over his more than forty years of itinerate evangelism he averaged two sermons a day! An excellent administrator, though sometimes dictatorial, he was continually exhorting his force of circuit riders, breaking ground for new churches, scurrying from one important meeting to another. He studied the Bible fervently, but also read other books. He arose early and accomplished so much that, were he on earth today, he would surely be sought after to conduct seminars on management and use of time.

When Asbury arrived in America in 1771, the Methodists numbered no more than a thousand. When he died in 1816, there were 214,000. Little wonder that he became the first Methodist bishop in America, a title, incidentally, that John Wesley deplored.

Journalist Herman B. Teeter aptly summed up Asbury's contribution to America:

"The names of Daniel Boone, Davy Crockett, Kit Carson, and Jim Bowie are well known in history and legend. Not so that of Francis Asbury. Yet the ex-blacksmith from England outlasted and outdistanced them all. He knew more hardship and physical suffering, but sought no personal fortune, no acclaim, no territory. Year after year he gathered behind him a growing army of hard-riding, hard-preaching men who, like himself, would never know comfort or riches.

"He must have faced more inclement weather in one year than most men brave in a lifetime.... His horses fell beneath him, or ran away with him. But people were his main concern. To him they were souls to be saved.... Asbury did the job he set out to do, and in his old age his passing to and fro across the land found thousands gathering for a glimpse of him. 'People call me by name as they pass me on the road, and I hand them a religious tract in German or English; or I call at a door for a glass of water, and leave a little pamphlet.'

"He never had a home of his own. He had no address other than 'America,' but sooner or later a letter so addressed would reach him.

"Today highways and railways crisscross the large slice of the United States that was Asbury country. Fly over it in a jet plane and look down on this vast area, once uncivilized and virtually uncharted. Even from 30,000 feet it stretches out of sight beyond every horizon. Try driving through Asbury country for 5,000 miles—a typical annual circuit for the pioneer bishop—and consider what it would be like to make the same trip by horseback, sulky, chaise, and afoot!"[3]

Asbury lamented the tendency of the early Methodist preachers to stay "shut up" in cities along the Eastern seaboard. He vowed at the outset to train a whole new generation of men—both preachers and laymen—who would move out beyond the four walls of their churches, follow the new westward population trends, and move among those people where the spiritual vacuum seemed greatest.

The man, his method, and his mission set forth an example that twentieth-century Christians might well follow today.

NINE

NOAH WEBSTER

THE IVY LEAGUE COLLEGES of an earlier era, most of them at one time evangelical in purpose, turned out a long parade of graduates who rose to prominence in law, politics, education, and other fields. They played a great part in shaping the heart and mind of America during its formative years.

One of the names most remembered today is Noah Webster, simply because his name has endured along with his dictionary still used (updated many times, of course) by millions.[1]

A graduate of Yale, Webster achieved distinction in many arenas. He practiced law in Hartford, launched a daily newspaper in New York, helped establish Amherst College, and routinely rubbed shoulders with men like George Washington, Alexander Hamilton, and John Jay.

But the biggest segment of his life—thirty-six

years of it in fact—he dedicated to the Herculean task of producing his *American Dictionary*.

Like a human computer, Webster systematized in his mind and in his huge files of clippings, almost every piece of knowledge he acquired. He meticulously researched everything from the cause of Asiatic cholera to the reasons for a seeming change in the American climate. He wrote on a wide spectrum of subjects, from the foundations of government and the laws of nations to the science of banking and the history of his country. But he specialized in pursuing the etymology of words.

No less a person could have ever completed the mammoth task he had undertaken and done it right. Even then English speech was changing rapidly from year to year, with new discoveries in science, new political terms, and a myriad of other forces upon the language.

At one point in the project, Webster suspended his labors on defining words and devoted a number of years on a related pursuit: tracing the origin of the English language and its connection with those of other countries. He researched the vocabularies of twenty of the principal languages of the world, and made a synopsis of the most important words in each.

Webster, after his extensive research on the origin of "language," sharply opposed the evolutionary concept that language *evolved* along with the progressive development of animal life from "grunts to groans."

Noah Webster obviously applied a Christian perspective to his study of languages. From his youth he respected religion, took a high view on the inspiration of the Scriptures, and set out from Yale to pursue a course of virtue through life—to perform every moral and social duty with scrupulous exactness.

But at the age of forty he began to confide that perhaps he was resting his beliefs more on his accomplishments than on the simple grace of God. He had been earnest in his endeavors and active for social good. But was this enough?

At this point he took up an earnest study of the Bible, with the same meticulous care and complete honesty that characterized the man himself. And as he advanced, his objections to the simple Gospel fell one by one, and one evening he cast himself down before God, confessed his sins, and implored pardon through the merits of the Redeemer alone.

The next morning he called his family together and, with deep emotion, told them that for years he had neglected one of his most important duties as their parent and head—family prayer. After reading the Scriptures he led his family to the throne of grace, a habit he continued until his death years later. He made a public profession in April, 1808, and three daughters soon followed with decisions of their own.

Webster continued in his daily study of the Scriptures over the years, despite the demands on his time in completing the *American Dictionary*, and certain definitions in those earlier editions reflect his Christian stance.

The tall, slender Noah Webster walked with a light and elastic step until the time of his death at eighty-five. As he faced the close of life on earth, Webster quoted to a friend the words of the apostle Paul: "I know whom I have believed, and am persuaded that he is able to keep that which I have committed unto him against that day."

TEN

FRANCIS SCOTT KEY

IT WAS AUGUST, 1814, and British troops had just raided the city of Baltimore, at that time the nation's capital city. On false charges they arrested a prominent physician of Upper Marlborough, Dr. Beanes, and took him captive. Friends of the doctor appealed to lawyer Francis Scott Key to try to secure his release.[1]

President James Madison gave a green light to the move. With an associate, Key set out in the United States cartel ship *Minden*. They overtook the British fleet and secured a promise from British Admiral Cochrane that the prisoner would be freed. But the American party was detained on board, pending a naval attack on Baltimore.

The British launched their attack on Fort McHenry, which defended naval access to the city. Key and his party watched the bombardment anxiously. From their position they could see clearly the American flag that flew over the fort.

Night fell and Key's comrades, utterly fatigued, retired below. But not Key himself. Through the night he watched "the rockets red glare, the bombs bursting in air." Toward morning the firing ceased. Had the fort fallen? Key paced the deck in an agony of suspense.

At "dawn's early light" his straining gaze caught sight of the flag. It was still there! From his pocket he took an old letter, the only piece of paper he could find. It was so small he could only write in abbreviated note form those immortal lyrics to "The Star Spangled Banner."

After sunrise the British admiral released the American ship. Back at Baltimore, Key wrote out the song in full and then showed it to Judge Nicholson, his brother-in-law, who had commanded a volunteer company of artillery in the fight. The judge was so impressed with it that the song was given promptly to a printer, who ran off copies in handbill form for distribution on the street. A musician, Ferdinand Durang, picked up a copy, caught the spirit of the lines and adopted the words to the tune of "Anacreon in Heaven." Soon the whole city took up the song, and passed it on to the nation.

Many may know this story, but most do not know that Francis Scott Key was also an evangelical Christian. He taught a Bible class for boys and for several decades up to his death he served as a vice-president of the American Sunday School Union, which planted thousands of Sunday schools across the nation in those early years.

In 1819 Francis Scott Key wrote another song, obviously not so widely known as our national anthem. It is still found in some hymnals, and it reveals the depth of his faith.

> Lord, with glowing heart I'd praise Thee,
> For the bliss Thy love bestows,
> For the pardoning grace that saves me,
> And the peace that from it flows;
> Help, O God, my weak endeavor;
> This dull soul to rapture raise;
> Thou must light the flame, or never
> Can my love be warmed to praise.

To a friend in Congress, Key, who also served as a United States district attorney in Washington, once wrote this message:

"If you are convinced you are a sinner, that Christ alone can save you from the sentence of condemnation; if you make an unconditional surrender of yourself to His service, He will in no wise cast you out."

In America today are still those who, like Key, are not afraid to express their patriotism, but who also know that the destiny of individuals, and, yes, the destiny of a nation, rest upon a commitment to Jesus Christ.

ELEVEN

ABRAHAM LINCOLN

THE YEAR, 1863. The United States of America, still less than one hundred years old, faced its greatest crisis. A great civil war threatened to destroy the Union as armies of the North and South clashed across the Potomac from Washington, D.C. and also to the southwest near Chatanooga, Tennessee.

The Senate called upon President Lincoln to set aside a national day of "fasting, humiliation and prayer." The President concurred and designated April 30. He urged both personal and national repentance.

"It is the duty of nations as well as of men," he said, "to own their dependence upon the overruling power of God, to confess their sins and transgressions, in humble sorrow, yet with assured hope that genuine repentance will lead to mercy and pardon; and to recognize the sublime truth, announced in the Holy Scriptures and proven by all history, that those nations only are blessed whose God is the Lord."[1]

Lincoln's proclamation continued with an analysis of the country which rings strangely true of our nation today:

"We have been the recipients of the choicest bounties of Heaven. We have been preserved, these many years, in peace and prosperity. We have grown in numbers, wealth and power, as no other nation has ever grown. But we have forgotten God. We have forgotten the gracious hand which preserved us in peace, and multiplied and enriched and strengthened us; and we have vainly imagined, in the deceitfulness of our hearts, that all these blessings were produced by some superior wisdom and virtue of our own. Intoxicated with unbroken success, we have become too self-sufficient to feel the necessity of redeeming and preserving grace, too proud to pray to the God that made us!"[2]

No other President so consistently demonstrated, and so deeply believed as did Abraham Lincoln that the almighty God of the universe rules in the affairs of men. Lincoln once said to his register of the treasury, L. E. Chittenden: "That the Almighty does make use of human agencies, and directly intervenes in human affairs, is one of the plainest statements of the Bible. I have had so many evidences of

His direction, so many instances when I have been controlled by some other power than my own will, that I cannot doubt that this power comes from above."[3]

The man who had just issued the Emancipation Proclamation concluded with the deep conviction, "I am confident that it is His design to restore the Union. He will do it in His own good time. We should obey and not oppose His will."[4]

Even as a boy, Lincoln seemed to grasp the great truth that God directs history. But he did wrestle with certain other doctrines of the Christian faith, especially in the days when he served as a young lawyer in New Salem, Illinois. Was Abraham Lincoln an orthodox Christian? What did he really believe? Why did he never join a church? Did he fall short in his doctrine and believe in universal salvation, that ultimately Jesus Christ would save all men? How did he regard the authority of the Bible?

Such questions about Abraham Lincoln have been researched, debated, and explored for years. Not everyone has come to the same conclusions. It is not my intent to try to settle the matter. But even a brief look at Lincoln overwhelms one with his obvious awareness of his need and dependence on One higher than himself.

From his boyhood log-cabin days Lincoln learned to study and memorize the Scriptures, both from his mother and perhaps also from listening to sermons at the Pigeon Creek Baptist Church. He once told a gathering of Black people who had given him a costly Bible in Baltimore, "All the good the Saviour gave to the world was communicated through this book. But for it we could not know right from wrong."[5]

And on another occasion he told his treasurer Chittenden:

"The character of the Bible is easily established, at least to my satisfaction. We have to believe many things which we do not comprehend. The Bible is the only one that claims to be God's book—to comprise His law—His history. It contains an immense amount of evidence of its own authenticity.... I decided a long time ago that it was less difficult to believe that the Bible was what it claimed to be than to disbelieve it."[6]

Abraham Lincoln knew his Bible well, and he could quote it with ease. The Scriptures permeate his speeches, not just as an adornment to impress others, but as an integral part of his logic. The biblical phrase, "a house divided against itself cannot stand," became his classic plea for preservation of the Union. His second

inaugural address is filled with the flavor of
King James rhetoric.

But during his days in New Salem, Lincoln
clearly struggled with his faith—or lack of
it—and it seems evident that at that time, at
least, he held a view of universal salvation—
from his misinterpretation of such verses as 1
Corinthians 15:22.

Because of this, perhaps, his political oppo-
nent for Congress at that time, Methodist circuit
rider Peter Cartwright, went so far as to label
him an "infidel." The term was popular in those
days, though often misused. Lincoln defended
himself in a handbill to the editor of the *Illinois
Gazette*. He denied he was an "open scoffer at
Christianity" and, in fact, said he could not
support a man for office whom he knew to be an
open enemy of, and scoffer at, religion.

Throughout his life Abraham Lincoln did not
join a church. Nor did he care for creeds. He
preferred to draw his convictions directly from
the Scriptures rather than from what he regarded as man-made abstracts.

It is unmistakable, however, that Abraham
Lincoln's spiritual convictions deepened as he
assumed the awesome role of President and
faced the agonizing dilemmas of the slavery
issue and a civil war.

The slavery question troubled Lincoln immensely. He firmly saw it as a moral evil, an injustice that would surely bring the wrath of God upon the nation. Common sense, coupled with the Bible he so frequently read, drove him to these conclusions. Yet there were those who, from the same Scriptures, insisted that the Bible did not specifically condemn slavery. They pointed to its existence, both in the Old and New Testament, that slaves were enjoined to be obedient to their masters, and that Paul himself sent the fugitive slave Onesimus back to his master Philemon at Colosse.

But Lincoln observed that the kind of slavery that existed in the culture of those times involved no racial overtones. Would not the advocates of slavery in America maintain that the slavery of a Black man was right, but the slavery of a white man wrong? And he wondered how a society could do to a whole race of men what they would have no man do to their own race.

Lincoln's first inaugural address on March 4, 1861, expressed a deep conviction that the God of history would overrule impending events to bring about His will.

"If the Almighty Ruler of nations," he said, "with his eternal truth and justice, be on your side of the North, or on yours of the South, that truth, and that justice will surely prevail, by the judgment of this great tribunal, the American people."[7]

Four years later, with the outcome of the Civil War tilting in favor of the Union, he once more hammered home, in his second inaugural address, the truth that "The Almighty has his own purposes."

In office Lincoln seemed to turn ever more to the Bible and to prayer. And with Lincoln, religion came from the depths of his soul. Any attempt to use religion simply for political advantage or to impress people of his piousness contradicted the very character and integrity of Abraham Lincoln.

Schuyler Colfax, who would eventually become vice-president of the United States, said Lincoln would often get up as early as four o'clock in the morning in order that he might have time to read his Bible and pray before visitors would begin to arrive at the White House.

Lincoln once told an intimate newspaper friend, Noah Brooks: "I have been driven many times upon my knees by the overwhelming conviction that I had nowhere else to go."[8]

During the Civil War, Lincoln originated a gigantic plan called the Sanitary Commission to care for the sick and wounded soldiers. It proved very successful. When Dr. John D. Hill, a prominent Buffalo physician and member of the commission, later complimented the President for conceiving such an idea, Lincoln replied:

"You must carry your thanks to a Higher Being. One stormy night I tossed on my bed, unable to sleep as I thought of the terrible sufferings of our soldiers and sailors. I spent an hour in agonizing prayer to God for some method of relief, and he put the Sanitary Commission in my mind, with all its details, as distinctly as though the instructions had been written out by pen and handed to me. Hereafter, always thank your heavenly Father, and not me, for this organization, which has eased so much pain and saved so many lives."[9]

But perhaps one of the most striking stories of Lincoln and prayer—and one of the best documented—surrounds the Battle of Gettysburg.

In a Washington hospital Lincoln stood at the bedside of General Sickles, who had just had his leg amputated due to a wound at Gettysburg. Sickles asked the President whether he had been anxious about the battle at Gettysburg. General James Rusling, who was also with the President, told of the conversation:

" 'No, I was not; some of my Cabinet and many others in Washington were, but I had no fears.' General Sickles inquired how this was, and seemed curious about it. Mr. Lincoln hesitated, but finally replied: 'Well, I will tell you how it was. In the pinch of the campaign up there, when everybody seemed panic-stricken, and nobody could tell what was going to happen, oppressed by the gravity of our affairs, I went to my room one day, and I locked the door, and got down on my knees before Almighty God, and prayed to Him mightily for victory at Gettysburg. I told Him that this was His war, and our cause, His cause, but we couldn't stand another Fredericksburg or Chancellorsville. And I then and there made a solemn vow to Almighty God, that if He would stand by our boys at Gettysburg, I would stand by Him.... And after that (I don't know how it was, and I can't explain it), soon a sweet comfort crept into my soul that God Almighty had taken the whole business into his own hands and that things would go all right at Gettysburg.' "[10]

The President had been praying for Vicksburg, too, and he told Sickles that he believed "our heavenly Father is going to give us victory there too."

Word had not yet reached him that Vicksburg also had fallen—just the day before!

Some might feel that Lincoln's spiritual vow on victory at Gettysburg sounds like he was bargaining with God. And did he keep his vow?

If so, how? One source declares that when he went to Gettysburg and saw the graves of thousands of United States soldiers, he then and there consecrated himself to Jesus Christ. Mrs. Lincoln spoke of Gettysburg's profound effect upon her husband. Other sources believe he was about to make a public profession of faith at the time an assassin's bullet struck him down.

The debate on the particulars of Lincoln's faith will go on; yet no one disputes that long before Gettysburg, Lincoln fully realized and lived out the conviction that "the most High ruleth in the kingdom of men" (Daniel 4:32). The same verse says that God "giveth it to whomsoever he will." If the "Almighty Ruler of Nations" at that time in history had put the reins of leadership into the hands of a man of lesser integrity than Lincoln, the Union might have never survived.

TWELVE

DWIGHT L. MOODY

CHICAGO CAN NEVER ERASE the memory of the great disaster that befell her little more than one hundred years ago. On an October Sunday evening in 1871, ominous flames erupted on the city's South Side. By midnight the entire populace was fleeing in panic as the inferno swept northward block by block, reducing the city to ashes.

When the city courthouse bell began to ring out the alarm and the first fire engines hurried toward the scene, a prominent Chicagoan named D. L. Moody was just concluding a regular Sunday evening evangelistic service in his tabernacle on the Near North Side.[1] Hearing the confusion outside, he and his soloist, Ira D. Sankey, promptly dismissed the capacity crowd. Hundreds in the gathering rushed to the aid of others or their own families.

As Moody made his way toward his own home, hurricanelike southwest winds from the fire blew sparks down around him, touching off first one house, then another. "The city's doomed," he said to his wife, Emma, as he walked in his front door.

The Moodys thought their own home was far enough from the blaze to escape, but in the early morning hours police knocked and urged them to leave. The parents sent their two children to the suburbs with a neighbor and began gathering up a few of their belongings.

Among them was a cherished portrait of D. L. Moody by the most famous portrait artist of the day. G. P. A. Healy had given it to him upon Moody's return from Great Britain, where he later staged a dramatically successful campaign that moved the hearts of more than a million people. His wife urged him to save the painting.

" 'Take my own picture!' he laughed. 'Well, that would be a joke. Suppose I meet some friends in the same trouble as ourselves, and they say, "Hullo Moody, glad you have escaped; what's that you have saved and cling to so affectionately?" Wouldn't it sound well to reply, "Oh, I've got my own portrait!" ' "[2]

Moody wouldn't touch it, but looters already on the scene obligingly cut it out of its frame and handed it to his wife.

It was not in the character of Dwight L. Moody to glory in himself, but rather, to glory in what God could do for the man who put his trust in Jesus Christ.

The great Chicago fire destroyed Moody's home, his church, and even the impressive Chicago YMCA he had launched, but in Moody's eyes it was not the worst catastrophe that could happen to man. It would be far worse that anyone should not hear clearly the Gospel of salvation.

By the time of the Chicago fire, Moody had already preached Jesus Christ to tens of thousands in America. But by the time of his death more than a quarter century later, some would estimate his total audience as high as one hundred million. And the impact of the Chicago Bible Institute he founded would resound around the world in the century to come.

Moody's spiritual life started in the back of a shoe store in Boston in 1855 when a dry-goods salesman named Edward Kimball, who also happened to be Moody's Sunday school teacher, led him to Jesus Christ.

Kimball afterward thought he had made a rather weak plea, but the next morning Moody "thought the old sun shone brighter than it ever had before. I thought that it was just smiling upon me. As I walked upon Boston Common and heard the birds singing in the trees, I thought they were all singing a song to me. Do you know how I fell in love with the birds? I had never cared for them before. It seemed to me that I was in love with all creation—I had not a bitter feeling against any man, and I was ready to take all men to my heart."[3]

Before long, Moody, who had little education, went west to Chicago and established himself as a first-rate shoe salesman. He invested in real estate and soon began to amass a small fortune. He could well have become a millionaire, said close friends, but the Wall Street panic of 1857 convinced him he should not regard faith as primarily "an aid to fortune."

Meanwhile, Moody had also been rounding up street urchins from the poor section of Chicago's North Side, and before long his burgeoning mission Sunday school hosted hundreds weekly. Darting from one house or shanty to the next, he left others breathless in his dogged pursuit of prospects. At one point his class met in an old dance hall, another time in an abandoned freight car. Often he would ride around the streets on a pony, with an ample supply of maple sugar or apples to hand out as an encouragement for boys and girls to attend his class. The children loved him.

Daily Moody pressed almost everyone he met

in Chicago with the question, "Are you a Christian?" One by one, people were converted.

The Sunday school work grew. Eventually Moody made a Chicago banker the superintendent, then later his good friend John V. Farwell, at the time Chicago's wealthiest retail merchant (who would later be overtaken by Marshall Field), accepted the position. In 1860 President-elect Abraham Lincoln visited Moody's class. Before he left he told the young urchins, "I was once as poor as any boy in the school, but I am now President of the United States, and if you attend to what is taught you here, some one of you may yet be President of the United States."[4]

Moody eventually gave up his flourishing shoe business and never again accepted a salary. Rather, he launched out on simple faith in every Christian venture he undertook. Time and again when funds were nonexistent, he saw God answer prayer. He rubbed shoulders frequently with millionaires, among them his good friend Cyrus McCormick, inventor of the harvester, who helped Moody establish the Chicago YMCA movement and gave liberally to it. Later McCormick's son, Cyrus, Jr., would become one of the first trustees of the Moody Bible Institute.

While at an international YMCA convention in Indianapolis in 1870, Moody was thrilled by the singing of a government revenue worker from Pennsylvania named Ira Sankey. After hearing Sankey sing with great pathos, "There Is a Fountain Filled with Blood," Moody urged him to join the Chicago ministry. Sankey finally agreed, but on a trial basis. Thus originated the Moody-Sankey team that would later take both America and Great Britain by storm.

By the summer of 1872 Chicago had begun to rise from the ashes, and a modest newly built 1,400-seat Moody Tabernacle served as a center of relief and evangelism. Then Dwight L. Moody took off on a visit to Great Britain. Among Christians he met there was a wholesale butcher named Henry Varley, who one day remarked casually to Moody that "the world has yet to see what God will do with a man fully consecrated to Him."

Moody thought about those words for weeks, and decided one day that, by God's power, he would be that man.

In the city of London alone the Moody-Sankey campaign reached an estimated 1.5 million and, seven years later, Moody's preaching mission at England's erudite Cambridge University would touch off a spiritual revival that would ultimately send hundreds of students around the world as missionaries.

Back home, America, too, needed Moody's

message, perhaps as never before. The Civil War, like all wars, had disrupted general morality. People chased after easy wealth. Corruption penetrated high political offices. Before launching a campaign in Philadelphia, Moody touched off a small revival at Princeton University. At Philadelphia one evening President Grant and several of his cabinet members sat on the platform. There was the New York campaign of 1876 and many more to follow in the cities and towns across America, spanning at least a quarter century until his death during a Kansas City campaign in 1899, just a few days before the turn of the twentieth century.

Many contend that Dwight L. Moody left his greatest legacy in 1886 when he established the Moody Bible Institute of Chicago.

The evangelist conceived the institution as a school to train Christian workers to reach Chicago. Moody called some of his friends to Chicago's Pacific Hotel in early 1887—among them Farwell, Cyrus McCormick, Jr., and lumber king T. W. Harvey—and founded the Chicago Evangelization Society.

But from China came a letter from C. T. Studd, Great Britain's famed athlete who had gone to China as a missionary following the Moody-sparked revival at Cambridge University. Studd had just inherited a part of his father's fortune (his famous sportsman father had also been converted under Moody). Studd enclosed $50,000 to start a Gospel work in north India, where the fortune had been made.

Moody could not honor that precise request but wrote Studd that he would do the next best thing and open a training school with it "from which men and women will go to all parts of the world to evangelize."

Soon afterward Moody spotted a lot next to his base of operations at Chicago Avenue and Wells Street and prayed that the Lord might provide that land for a school. In time God did, and also several other adjacent lots. Dormitories went up to house 200 men and 50 women. He named as its first superintendent Reuben A. Torrey, a Greek and Hebrew scholar who, although he had sat under "higher critics" in Germany, "returned wholeheartedly to believe in the Bible, the whole Bible, as the Word of God."

Moody also saw the need for religious books and established the Moody Colportage Association. He conceived the low-cost religious paperback for the masses at least a half century before the modern-day paperback came into its own.

Little could Moody have foreseen the tremendous and far-reaching impact the Moody

Bible Institute would have in the twentieth century: a vast, multifaceted world ministry that is still rapidly expanding.

It seems that wherever D. L. Moody went he set in motion, under God's power and wisdom, spiritual events that would eventually touch the ends of the earth.

" 'By-and-by,' he had said but a few months before [his death], 'you will hear people say, "Mr. Moody is dead." Don't you believe a word of it. At that very moment I shall be more alive than I am now…. I was born of the flesh in 1837, I was born of the Spirit in 1855. That which is born of the flesh may die. That which is born of the Spirit will live forever.' "[5]

CONCLUSION

As our nation celebrates its bicentennial and goes on to build for the future, what should these profiles say to each one of us?

These men of spiritual conviction—and there were many more—faced problems that were not unlike, in many ways, the issues that confront us today. Each reader will draw his own conclusions and make application, hopefully in the light of Scripture.

Let me suggest, however, at least three truths which seem to stand out.

One is that God rules in the affairs of men and that, in due time, the United States emerged as a world power, not by accident, but by design.

George Washington sensed this even at the outset. In his first inaugural address he declared:

"No people can be bound to acknowledge and adore the invisible hand which conducts the affairs of men more than the people of the United States. Every step by which they have advanced to the character of an independent nation seems to have been distinguished by some token of providential agency."

Abraham Lincoln constantly sought "the Almighty Ruler of Nations."

John Witherspoon, in his address to the Continental Congress on May 17, 1776, spoke on "The Dominion of Providence over the Affairs of Men."

Another truth comes across clearly: that a democracy, if it is to succeed, must rest on a strong moral base. Our Founding Fathers clearly understood this.

George Washington, in his farewell address, persuasively extolled religion as the ground from which morality takes its rise. He warned that "reason and experience both forbid us to expect that national morality can prevail in exclusion of religious principles."

When the United States Supreme Court in June, 1962, announced its now famous "regent's" prayer decision, far-reaching effects resounded across the land. It triggered a rash of lower court cases in which plaintiffs cited everything from classroom devotions and prayer at school milk break to baccalaureate services and even the Pledge of Allegiance itself as "unconstitutional." Some public school superintendents and principals, who feared the risk of local lawsuits, regarded the whole issue as a "hot potato" and hastened to silence all mention of God in the classroom. As one grade school principal told his teachers, "When you're in the classroom, you have no religion."

When man for the first time circled the surface of the moon just four days before Christmas in 1968, millions around the world watched and listened as astronaut Frank Borman read from the creation account in the opening chapter of Genesis, "In the beginning God...." An infuriated Madalyn Murray O'Hair has been trying unsuccessfully ever since to secure an official government "censure."

At the crux of the crisis, of course, is the First Amendment to the U.S. Constitution, which states that "Congress shall make no law respecting an establishment of religion or prohibiting the free exercise thereof."

The debate has focused around this passage of sixteen words. Theologians have wrestled with it, historians have explained it, lawyers have interpreted it—with different shades of viewpoint. While admittedly the issues are complex, it is beyond dispute that the Founding Fathers wanted to prohibit any chance of a state church (or church-state), either at the state or national level.

But it is just as clear that they did not wish to

silence the voices of Christian conviction, nor "relegate God" to the extreme perimeters of the American system.

Who, then, is really undermining the Constitution? Certainly not those who wish to retain that spirit behind its inception: that God is supreme and that our democracy must stand on this assumption.

Would not the real danger lie with those who are waving piously the "establishment of religion" clause while glossing over the second part of that same amendment they allege to defend? For that amendment not only rules against the establishment of religion, but also against "prohibiting the free exercise thereof."

The men profiled in this book who "helped make America" teach us at least one more great lesson for our day. Each one of them made an astounding impact on those around him, and on the nation. Their influence has resounded through the decades, and will still be felt in generations to come.

Of Christians in particular, it has always been true that they have exercised an influence on society far beyond their numbers. Today our nation may appear at times to be on the verge of collapse. Many throw up their hands and cry, "What's the use?" But great was the crisis also when Samuel Adams cried out for liberty, when

Jonathan Edwards preached for revival, when Abraham Lincoln called for preservation of the Union.

It takes only a handful of dedicated men—in the right time, at the right place—to change the course of human events. The Gospel of itself has great power. One Christian with the message of Jesus Christ can change one life, or perhaps only a handful of lives, and see his influence eventually multiply to change other lives, and even society itself.

Had not Christians of the past set great spiritual forces in motion and reversed the inevitable degeneracy in the hearts of men, the United States even by now may have collapsed.

Let every American Christian become the salt of the earth and the salt of his nation.

NOTES

CHAPTER 1

1. See Samuel Eliot Morrison, "Christopher Columbus, Mariner," *American Heritage*, Dec. 1955, p. 72-95.
2. August J. Kling, "The Christopher Columbus That Few People Know," *Moody Monthly*, Oct. 1972, p. 27.
3. Christopher Columbus, "Libro de las Profecias" in *Raccolta di documenti e studi* (Rome: Italian Ministry of Public Ed., 1894), as translated by Kling, pp. 68-69.
4. Kling, p. 68.

CHAPTER 2

1. Information concerning Bradford was obtained primarily from Verna Hall, comp., *The Christian History of the Constitution*, (San Francisco: Foundation for Amer. Chr. Ed., 1973).

CHAPTER 3

1. Francis Russell, "Apostle to the Indians," *American Heritage*, Dec. 1957, pp. 4-6.
2. Ibid. pp. 117-19.

CHAPTER 4

1. Verna Hall, comp., *The Christian History of the Constitution*, p. 266.
2. Ibid., pp. 268-69.
3. Ibid., pp. 267-68.
4. Ibid., p. 266.

CHAPTER 5

1. Verna M. Hall, comp., *The Christian History of the Constitution*, p. 332.
2. Ibid., p. 351.
3. Ibid., p. 332.

4. Russell T. Hitt, ed., *Heroic Colonial Christians* (Philadelphia: Lippincott, 1966), pp. 228-29.
5. Ibid., p. 346.

CHAPTER 6

1. Information concerning Witherspoon was obtained primarily from Russell T. Hitt, ed., *Heroic Colonial Christians*, pp. 226, 232-33. Used by permission.

CHAPTER 7

1. Russell T. Hitt, ed., *Heroic Colonial Christians*, p. 13.
2. Ibid., pp. 32-33.
3. Ibid., p. 55.
4. William Warren Sweet, *The Story of Religion in America* (New York: Harper, 1950), p. 129.
5. Ibid., p. 130.

CHAPTER 8

1. Information concerning Asbury was obtained primarily from Herman B. Teeter, "The Incredible Francis Asbury," *Together*, Aug.-Sept. 1971, pp. 27-36.
2. Ibid., p. 31.
3. Ibid., p. 36.

CHAPTER 9

1. Information concerning Webster was obtained primarily from Rosalie J. Slater, *Teaching and Learning America's Christian History* (San Francisco: Foundation for Amer. Chr. Ed., 1973), pp. 280-97.

CHAPTER 10

1. Information concerning Key was obtained primarily from Galbraith Hall Todd, *The Torch and the Flag*, (Philadelphia: Sunday School Union, 1966).

CHAPTER 11

1. *The Collected Works of Abraham Lincoln*, as quoted by William J. Wolf, *The Almost Chosen People* (Garden City, N.Y.: Doubleday, 1959), pp. 162-63.
2. Ibid., pp. 163-64.
3. L. E. Chittenden, *Recollections of President Lincoln and His Administration*, as quoted by Wolf, p. 156.
4. Chittenden, as quoted by Clarence E. Macartney, *Lincoln and the Bible* (New York: Abingdon-Cokesbury, 1949), p. 27.
5. *The Collected Works of Abraham Lincoln*, as quoted by Wolf, p. 135.
6. Chittenden, as quoted by Macartney, pp. 54-55.
7. Wolf, pp. 115-16.
8. Noah Brooks in *Harper's Monthly*, July 1865, as quoted by Wolf, p. 125.
9. *The Globe* (New York City), Feb. 13, 1911; as quoted in William J. Johnstone, *How Lincoln Prayed* (New York: Abingdon, 1931), p. 87.
10. James F. Rusling, *Men and Things I Saw in Civil War Days*, as quoted by Wolfe, p. 125.

CHAPTER 12

1. Information concerning Moody was obtained primarily from J. C. Pollock, *Moody: A Biographical Portrait of the Pacesetter in Modern Mass Evangelism* (New York: Macmillan, 1963).
2. William R. Moody, *D. L. Moody* (New York: Macmillan, 1930), pp. 126-27.
3. Ibid., p. 35.
4. Pollock, p. 42.
5. Edward L. Pell, *Dwight L. Moody* (Richmond, Va.: B. F. Johnson, 1900), p. 272.